The Amazing A–Z of Resilience

First edition published in hardback in Great Britain in 2021 by Jessica Kingsley Publishers
This paperback edition published in Great Britain in 2022 by Jessica Kingsley Publishers
An Hachette Company

1

Copyright © David Gumbrell 2021, 2022
Illustrations copyright © Vanand Andresian 2021, 2022

All rights reserved. No part of this publication may be reproduced, stored in a retrieval system, or transmitted, in any form or by any means without the prior written permission of the publisher, nor be otherwise circulated in any form of binding or cover other than that in which it is published and without a similar condition being imposed on the subsequent purchaser.

A CIP catalogue record for this title is available from the British Library and the Library of Congress

ISBN 978 1 83997 337 6
eISBN 978 1 78775 367 9

Printed and bound in Great Britain by Ashford Colour Press

Jessica Kingsley Publishers' policy is to use papers that are natural, renewable and recyclable products and made from wood grown in sustainable forests. The logging and manufacturing processes are expected to conform to the environmental regulations of the country of origin.

Jessica Kingsley Publishers
Carmelite House
50 Victoria Embankment
London EC4Y 0DZ

www.jkp.com

The Amazing A–Z of Resilience

26 Curious Stories and Activities to Lift Yourself Up

David Gumbrell

Jessica Kingsley Publishers
London and Philadelphia

Dedicated to E and Z –

two important letters in my alphabet

Introduction

Sometimes people say, when you go on a journey, that you are going from 'A to B'.

This book is an 'A to Z' journey if you read it in alphabetical order. Along the way you will encounter many curious facts, lots of things to make you think and 26 activities that you can have a go at.

Alternatively, you might like to jump around a bit. Maybe start with the initial letters of your name, rather than A (although your name might start with A – it might be Arianna, Audley or Ainsley). So, for me, I might start with the chapter 'D is for Daisy Chains' and then move on to the chapter 'G is for Grandparents'; it is up to you.

Resilience is about recognising when things are not right and doing something about it (rather than pretending that it is not happening). Instead of hiding, we need to seek help when we are struggling, or try to figure it out for ourselves. Life can be tricky at times, but we need to deal with things when they come up.

Although the chapters are linked by the theme of resilience, they do not follow from A to B to C…so feel free to dip in and read a chapter, take time to think about what it is saying, try the art activity and then move on to another letter, another day.

The Amazing A–Z of Resilience is also a book to be shared. You can read it with a friend, a parent, a grandparent, or in class with your teacher. A walk in the countryside is more fun if you are with other people. Similarly, this journey is good if you can share it with others.

And why are there so many Zs in the title of the final chapter? The reason is that our sleep is **SO** important. It really helps us to rest and recover and to be more resilient. You can read more about this in the chapter

'ZZZ is for Sleep', but if you do just one thing better – get some sleep!

We also need to look after ourselves better. Resilience is about caring for yourself and being compassionate to yourself, being as kind to yourself as you are to your friends and family. This means exercising, having a hobby, eating well and, yes, you've got it, getting a good night's sleep.

Along your journey you are going to meet Paddington Bear, a Canadian dinosaur called a Xenoceratops and a Roman god called Vulcan. You are going to learn about an amazing kite flier, pirates' treasure and which toys were taken to the International Space Station by the *Discovery* astronauts so that they could experiment with them. But most importantly, I want you to learn more about you!

This book, you see, is all about **YOU**, really. It is a guidebook for **YOUR** journey, not mine. Along the way, each new character can teach you something about **YOU**!

So sit back, relax and enjoy this excursion. Luckily, there will be an ice-cream stop somewhere on the way (depending on which route you take).

A is for Alphabetti Spaghetti

Do you love alphabetti spaghetti on toast, spelling out your name with the pasta letters in front of you? There are never enough of some letters, like Js, so you have to dig around to find them! Sometimes there aren't any of a letter you need, and you have to do something like turn an 'L' round the other way to make it look like a 'J', or put a short bit of spaghetti over an 'O' to make a 'Q'!

There are around 90 letters in each small tin, and therefore you can make a **LOT** of different words if you can unscramble the tomato-sauced letters. It's a bit like an anagram, isn't it? Muddled-up letters, rearranged to make a word.

Can you find a number within the word **SPAGHETTI**?

You've got the T and E for TEN, but not the N. How about other numbers?

Just stopping for a moment to think through how to unravel these letters is a good thing. You need to give yourself time to think things through before you come up with a solution. Not everything that is worth solving can be done immediately.

But challenging problems come with more rewarding solutions!

Alternatively, you can grab a piece of paper and start writing your thoughts down to start to organise them. If you can see your thoughts with your own eyes, then you can build on them to find that solution. If your thoughts still seem like unorganised spaghetti, then you can ask others for help, of course.

Have you got the anagram yet? (The answer is **EIGHT**!)

Why Not Try This?

Use an orange pencil to write down two tricky things that you are thinking about at the moment.

Put an arrow by each and then write next to them the first thing you could do to make them feel less tricky.

B
is for Balloon

Did you know that helium balloons are not just for birthdays? They are used to tell us about the weather too. Without weights attached to their ribbons, helium balloons will continue to rise and rise. If indoors, this means they float to the ceiling; if outside, it means up and up into the sky!

Up, up and up – in fact, so high that they pass birds and aeroplanes, through the clouds and about halfway to the edge of space! Weather balloons are very big, even on the ground, and get bigger as they rise! Eventually, they burst and anything that they were lifting falls back down to Earth. All the weather recording equipment does too, and therefore it has to be attached to a parachute for its downward journey!

On good days, you can feel like a buoyant balloon. The day is going to be great; you can't wait to get going, this is your moment, you have been waiting weeks for this. If you don't hold yourself back, you are going to keep rising and rising.

On other days, you might have something that is weighing you down. It might be a worrying thought, a concern about a piece of school work, or a friendship issue in the playground. You can feel a bit deflated, more like a balloon a week after the party.

Either way, it's OK. Sometimes you will feel lifted, at other times not; that is normal – just stay floating if you can!

Why Not Try This?

At the end of each day, ask yourself, 'What is the second-best thing that has happened to me today?' That will really make you think about at least two moments when you were floating like a helium balloon.

Maybe you could even keep a diary of these moments so that you can look back at them.

C

is for Conkers

(or maybe even Conquers?)

I've always wondered why conkers are called conkers.

It seems such a strange name when they come from a tree called a horse chestnut!

Maybe it's the difference between the name of the seed when it is on the tree (because that is what a conker is) and the name of the game that we play once the conker has been taken out of its spiky shell.

Some people think that it comes from 'conquer' – to beat someone in a battle; after all, you do battle each other, by hitting your conker against your opponent's, don't you?

Maybe it would be better to keep the conker in its shell for the battle – it does have spikes like some kind of medieval weapon!

Are you a bit like a conker? Do you sometimes feel that you have to wear a spiky outer shell, as a form of protection from someone? At times, this can be a good thing, especially if people are being unkind with their actions or their words.

At other times, however, it is good to be trusting and to let people past your shell and see the real you, the shiny precious 'conker' inside! Just as in the autumn, when the browning shell splits open, we glimpse a small part of the conker inside.

Who are the people who know the real you, beyond the spiky layer?

Who helps you when you feel the need for a spiky shell?

Why Not Try This?

Draw six conker shapes on a piece of paper – you can add the laces if you like, but don't colour the conkers in.

Inside three conkers write the names of people who know the real you.

In the other three conkers, write the names of people who help you when you need a spiky shell.

Keep all six somewhere safe to remind you of the real **YOU**!

D is for Daisy Chains

'To love them, to love them not' – daisies are often found on lawns, school fields and grassy verges. These simple, white-petalled flowers are both intriguing and everywhere!

What's your longest daisy chain, in one long, flowing line?

Also, do you know which famous girl, known for her adventures with a clock-watching rabbit, loved to make these natural necklaces and bracelets?

It was Alice, in her *Adventures in Wonderland*, who was known to like creating daisy chains. Even before her adventures with the White Rabbit began, she was thinking whether 'the pleasure of making a daisy chain would be worth the trouble of getting up and picking the daisies'.

Whilst she considers this, she is distracted when 'a White Rabbit ran close by her'. It is her decision to follow the rabbit and so we can assume that the daisy chain never even got started!

Sometimes, it is good to be on your own connecting daisies whilst thinking of other things. At moments like this we can relax and be ourselves; it is good to enjoy your own company, to be that unique daisy.

However, at other times, we need to have other people to help and support us, and to connect to like a daisy chain. You can also build longer chains by adding new people on to them. Making a new friend or working with a different person in school can extend the number of people that you are connected to.

Why Not Try This?

Make your own five-daisy chain by using five green cable ties for stems.

Draw a daisy flower, write your name on it and then stick it into position on the central cable tie.

Write your friends' names on the other four flowers around yours.

Each time you make a new friend, add another cable-tie daisy to your line.

E is for Easter Eggs

Before Easter eggs were made of chocolate, our popular hollow eggs were made of papier mâché! Like piñatas, they were made with paper soaked in glue because it is easier to shape. Soggy paper strips are simpler to bend and curve. Once dried, they keep their newly formed shapes, such as a donkey (in the case of a traditional Mexican piñata) or an egg (the traditional Easter shape).

It was the discovery of tempering chocolate (heating and cooling to very accurate temperatures) that finally strengthened the chocolate, allowing it to become crisp and shiny on setting. The chocolatier could now create Easter eggs!

Usually, the eggs are filled with some smaller sweets and then sealed and wrapped in foil, but sometimes they are left empty. You may recall a time when your stomach felt empty when you were hungry (especially when talking about chocolate). But you may also have felt hollow and empty in your mind; you can't give a reason, but you just feel blank.

If you are feeling like this, then you may just need some time to remind yourself of all the good things that you have in your life (the sweet treats inside of you). This can balance out the things that are not going so well (the ones that make you feel hollow). Sometimes it is easy to think of all the bad things that are happening and so we need to tell ourselves to concentrate on the good things.

Why Not Try This?

Find yourself a small plastic toy egg (the ones found in a popular chocolate treat).

Cut yourself five strips of kitchen foil and use a marker pen to write five things that are going well for you on them.

Fold each strip and keep them in your egg as a reminder. Wrap the whole thing in foil to keep it safe (and to make it look like an Easter egg, of course)!

F is for Face Paint

Face painting is practised all over the world. Not the pastel, glittery patterns that you may go for, but tribal face (and body) paintings have carefully chosen colours that have hidden (well, hidden to you) meanings behind them.

Traditional paint is usually made out of clay; yours could be made of cornflour, baby lotion and water (maybe with some glitter as well!). It is also coloured with natural ingredients; your face paint uses food colouring!

But which ingredients would make the strongest red?

Cranberries, strawberries, cherries on a fruit theme?

Or rose petals, tulips or saffron on a flower theme?

Face paint can allow you, for a short time at least, to be someone, or something, else. This can be a fun thing to do at a fair, as you can hide your real self and become a tiger or a butterfly. You can then wipe the face paint off and be back to your usual self. However, it can be much harder to cover up real emotions on your face, can't it?

When you are being your usual self (unpainted), other people can accurately judge how to react to you. That's why your face is so expressive – you can smile, you can frown, you can lower your bottom lip. Just like traditional face painting gives clues as to rank and status, your natural face gives clues as to how you are feeling. It is important for you to be able to recognise the emotions in others and for your friends to be able to see how you are feeling too.

Why Not Try This?

On a blank playing card or a piece of card of a similar size, draw an outline of a head shape.

Stick two googly eyes into position.

Now, roll out some playdough to make eyebrows, a mouth and a nose.

Can you create nine different faces and name the emotions that they are showing?

Maybe take a picture of each to make a 'Gallery of Feelings'.

G is for Grandparents

'If my family tree branches out from me, then does that make me the trunk or a twig?' That's what I asked my grandad the other day.

At first he smiled, and then went on to say, 'If you are a twig, then your parents are branches and that makes me, your grandad, the trunk?

'I say Grandad, but people call their grandparents by different names – there are family trees all over the world!

'In Germany, Grandma and I might be called O<u>ma</u> and O<u>pa</u> (you can see how the ma and pa bits are similar to grand<u>ma</u> and grand<u>pa</u>). In the Philippines, we might be called Lola and Lolo, or if we used Swahili names, then we'd be Bibi and Babu.

'I'll just stick to Grandad, the trunk of our family tree!'

I'm lucky that my grandparents boosted me up and made me feel like I was playing Jenga in reverse. They took the wooden bricks off the top and slid them back into the gaps. That made me feel less wobbly and more in control. The returned blocks made me feel more stable – I came home thinking that I was going to be all right, that my grandparents loved me for who I was and what I did.

This is called **unconditional love** – no conditions, no rules, just love. I was number one for the weekend, I could have treats, I could play old board games (and they let me win). I loved my grandparents.

Why Not Try This?

With Jenga blocks, or LEGO® blocks, make yourself a family tree.

Don't worry if the colours don't match – making it multi-coloured is good.

Then write your family's names on to white stickers and place them on the 'branches'.

This will remind you of all the people whom you love and who love you.

H is for Hall of Mirrors

'Bumpy mirror on the wall, how do you make me look so tall?'

Facing one kind of mirror, I can be tall (taller than I actually am); facing another, I can be short. One mirror can make your head shrink, whilst another can make your legs *eeellloonnggaattee* – it's so funny.

Some say that the first Hall of Mirrors was created in the Palace of Versailles, in France. It was a corridor of 17 mirrors and 17 windows which tricked the eye into thinking that the formal gardens of the palace were on both sides of the hall!

A Hall of Mirrors was also made famous by Charlie Chaplin – a famous funny man of silent black-and-white films. He was chased through the Hall of Mirrors by policemen, who became disorientated, unsure whether to go left or right, not knowing if Chaplin was going forwards or backwards!

Sometimes you can look in the mirror and say, 'Is that really *me*?' Or, 'Is that the *me* that people see?'

I guess that this is to be expected, as most of the time you 'see' yourself looking outwards, not looking inwards! Maybe you need to consider different questions:

Is this the real me?
Is this how other people see me?
Am I what I do, what I look like or what I say?

You are probably a mix of them all, but it would help you to shorten the time that you stand in front of a mirror and lengthen the time you focus on what is good about you and widen your experiences, because, in this 'Hall of Mirrors', you can stand tall.

Why Not Try This?

Think of three words that describe how awesome you are.

Write them as if they were stretched, or squashed by making them tall or repeating letters to eeellloonnggaattee them.

Now try looking in a mirror and reading them aloud.

'I am _____ , _____ and _____ . I am **ME**!'

I

is for I-Spy

Did you know that the very first I-Spy book had the title *I-Spy at the Seaside*?

The idea behind the books was that you ticked off each of the pictures and wrote the date that you 'spied it' in the book. However, spotting some of the things was tricky as they could be quite rare or easy to miss, or the tide might be in and therefore there were no rock pools in which to see limpets, crabs and sea anemones! So, if you did complete a whole page, that would be an achievement. To finish the whole book and to have spotted everything was worth the certificate you got for your perseverance. You just needed to send your completed book back to the publishers to claim your prize.

You may have some I-Spy books that you still take on car journeys? They are certainly good to get you to look, to be curious and to take notice of what is around you. Certainly, when we are on our mobile devices too much, we are living in a virtual world, rather than in the real one, aren't we!

Do you still love going to the seaside? The power of the waves, the spray of the water, the squawk of the seagulls. I haven't got an I-Spy book any more, but I have still kept my curiosity! You just need to ask '**WHY**?' – **Why** is the air salty? **Why** do seagulls make so much noise? Maybe the modern version of the books should be Why-Spy, rather than I-Spy!

Why Not Try This?

Think of a topic – it doesn't have to be the seaside.

Now ask yourself five questions beginning with 'Why'.

Try to find the answers on the internet, or by going to a library.

J is for Jelly

The instructions on the packet simply say, 'Just add hot water, stir till melted and then pour into a mould. Allow to cool.'

What it doesn't say on the packet is that jelly is amazing! It takes on the shape of any mould and can therefore become a layered tower, a fluted ring or even a triple dome-on-dome-on-dome structure.

In the past (before there was plastic) the moulds used to be made out of pottery or metals such as tin, copper or brass. They were highly elaborate designs and the finished jelly was the centrepiece of the table. No Victorian or Edwardian kitchen (which was the period in history when jelly became really popular) would be without a selection of jelly moulds for both sweet and savoury jellies! Yes, jelly for dinner, not just pudding!

The clear gelatine, the stuff that holds the jelly semi-solid, can be flavoured with meat juices and vegetables instead of the fruit juice, sugar and fruit that we know…yum!

One thing that will always be associated with jelly is that it is wobbly and sometimes we can be too. It can feel as if someone is shaking us and that we can't stop that wiggle. When you are feeling a bit wobbly, what (or who) helps you to 'get steady'? When we are feeling like this, we might be wise to think of the phrase 'Get set, go!' But rather than connecting it to races and going fast, I want you to think of it as 'Get set like a jelly, then go,' and slowing down. Remember, even jellies need time to cool and settle before they can stand calm on their own.

Why Not Try This?

Write a simple three-step recipe about how you can **reset** yourself when you are feeling wobbly.

Start each one with a verb – what are you going to **do**?

1.

2.

3.

K

is for Kite

'Roll up, roll up, win five dollars!'

This was the prize offered to anyone who could fly a kite across the gorge of the river by Niagara Falls, the world-famous waterfall. In the 1840s, they wanted to build a bridge but they couldn't find a way to get the first cable across the gap of around 240 metres. Step forward a 16-year-old boy with an ability to fly kites!

With two guide ropes attached, Homan Walsh managed to stand on the Canadian side of the river and fly his kite to the American side. One guide rope was then attached to a tree whilst the second rope was sent back across the gorge, and so on. Eventually, what began as a skilled kite flight ended as a rather impressive suspension bridge connecting Canada and the United States.

Who would have thought that a kite-flying competition would lead to the building of a bridge? Congratulations, Homan, you deserved your 150 dollars (what the prize would be worth today).

Many adults didn't think that the problem could be solved, but Homan did. Through perseverance (it took several attempts over eight days to make it work), he solved a problem that the grown-ups were struggling with. The solution was not the most obvious one, but sometimes that is the case. We need to try to think in a different way, to be creative with our ideas and to be confident enough to put these ideas forward. Like a kite, sometimes we need to weave and meander to find the right path.

Why Not Try This?

Sometimes problems need innovative solutions – and this problem does.

Find yourself three pencils – it doesn't matter what colour they are.

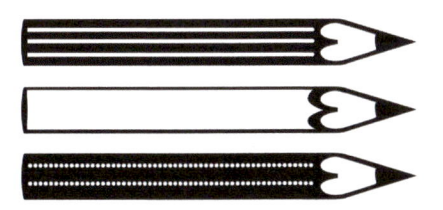

Problem – make these three pencils into six (no breaking them in half).

Clue – think like a Roman!

(Go to the bottom of page 62 to find out the answer.)

L

is for Ladybirds

Are all ladybirds – or ladybugs as Americans call them – red with black spots?

No, they are not! (Although many people think that they are.)

There are red ladybirds, but there are also orange and yellow ones.

There are some that have black spots, but also ones with black shells and coloured spots.

All of these colours do have one thing in common, though: they are all there to warn a predator that they won't taste very nice if they eat them. It is a defensive trait to keep themselves alive – it's like saying, stay away, swift (a bird that likes a ladybird snack) – **I'm yucky**!

So, if you count the spots, you can tell the age of a ladybird, right?

Most ladybirds from one family will have very similar numbers of spots. So, rather than telling its age, they help you to work out which ladybird family it is part of. For example, the seven-spot ladybird (the red one that comes to mind when we think 'ladybird') is not seven years old; no ladybird is that old – they usually only live for a year.

If the threatening colours of the ladybird don't have the desired effect, then their dotty wing cases open up and allow them to fly away. Sometimes we can feel worried about something to the point that we want to unfurl our wings and take flight too. It is at times like these that we can feel scared about what is going to happen. This can build up in our minds and it can become much bigger than it actually is. What do you do in these situations? What works best for you?

Why Not Try This?
Find yourself some round pebbles or stones.

Paint them in ladybird colours (remember, not just red).

On the underside of each, write yourself a message about how to be strong.

M

is for Mini Golf

A windmill, a rollercoaster and a castle gatehouse?

In Victorian times it was not seen as very 'lady-like' to be playing a full round of golf, so the famous St Andrews club in Scotland created a 'gentler' game that we would describe as putting. However, one thing was missing – obstacles like water hazards and bunkers. Soon after, a game called 'Gofstacle' was advertised in *The Illustrated London News* with the headline 'Bridge, Stick, Tunnel and Box: a golf game for putters'. Had the popular newspaper of the time announced the first ever mini golf?

In America they'd invented a game too, with tyres, barrels and pipes as their obstacles. The surface of crushed cottonseed hulls was a bit bumpier than a grass lawn, but that all added to the fun and excitement. Soon the crazy-golf phenomenon was born and tyres became turrets, barrels became windmills and drainpipes became bridges. Crazy golf is still alive and well today.

You record the number of shots you take on your scorecard against the par for the hole (the number of shots they suggest it will take to get the ball in the hole), using a small pencil, if provided. On some holes you may take more shots (above par), on others fewer (below par). Sometimes adults use these phrases to describe how they are feeling. 'I'm feeling below par today' means that they don't feel quite themselves; they feel less than normal in terms of energy levels, happiness or feeling positive. Do you have days like this? The good news is **we all do**, it's not just you!

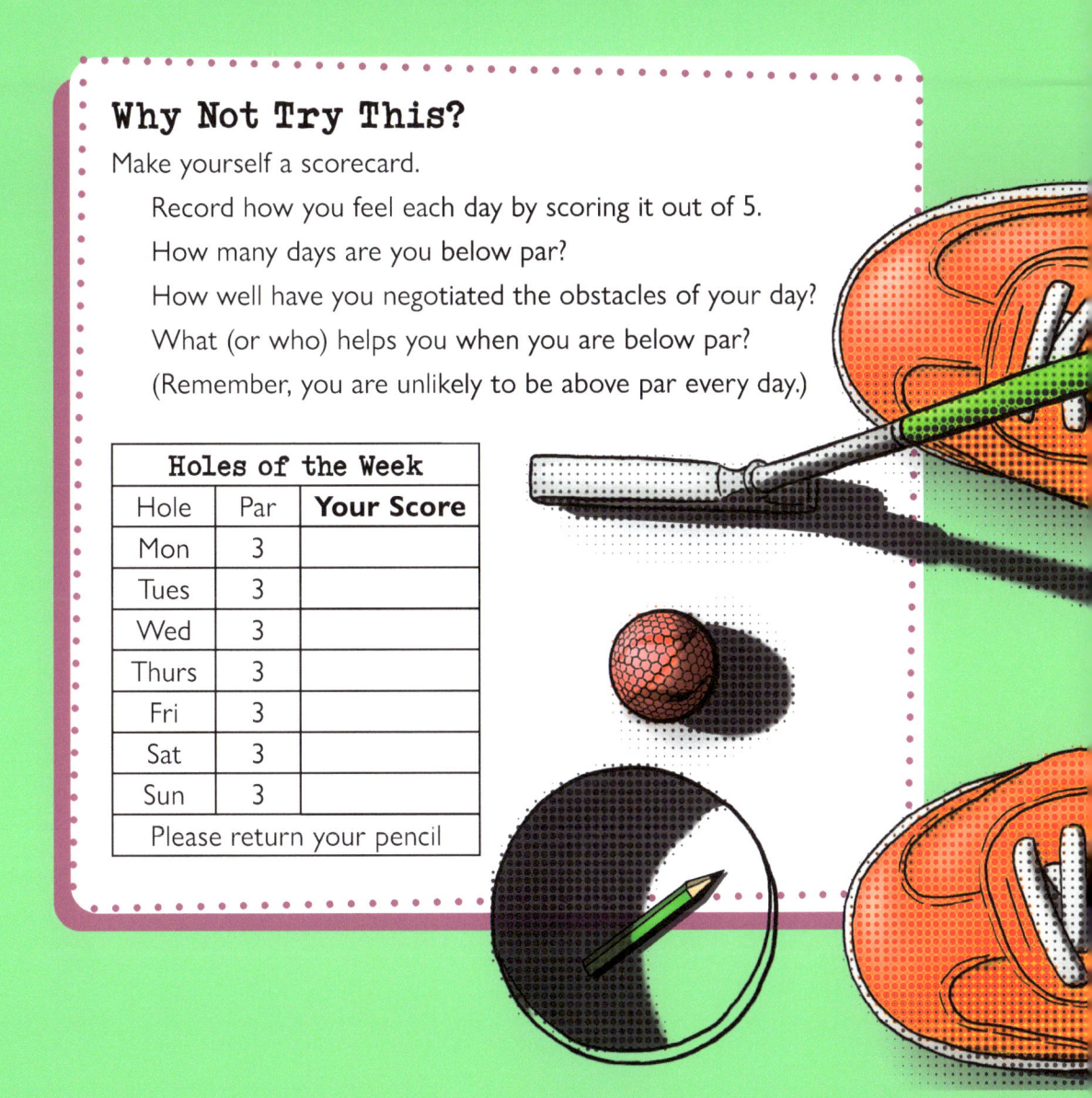

Why Not Try This?

Make yourself a scorecard.

> Record how you feel each day by scoring it out of 5.
> How many days are you below par?
> How well have you negotiated the obstacles of your day?
> What (or who) helps you when you are below par?
> (Remember, you are unlikely to be above par every day.)

Holes of the Week		
Hole	Par	**Your Score**
Mon	3	
Tues	3	
Wed	3	
Thurs	3	
Fri	3	
Sat	3	
Sun	3	
Please return your pencil		

N is for Neapolitan Ice Cream

Did you know that one in every three countries has a flag with three coloured bands?

Some have horizontal bands, such as Armenia, Myanmar and Luxembourg; others have vertical bands like Senegal and Mali. Italy even based the look of Neapolitan ice cream on the nation's flag of green, white and red bands. The red is strawberry (although more pink than red), the white is vanilla (although more yellow than white), and green is…chocolate (more brown than green)!

The reason for this is that the third ice cream used to be pistachio, made from pale green pistachio nuts. However, swapping the pistachio out for chocolate made sales of the ice cream go up and therefore green became brown and the connection to Italy's flag was forgotten… until now!

Just as there are three flavours in a Neapolitan ice cream, you also have three choices when you are faced with a tricky decision – flight, fight or freeze. When you freeze, for example, you might just be unsure what to do, so stopping can be good as it allows you time to think before you act. Give yourself a moment to consider what to do before you do it! In this way, you may build your strength to make decisions which are good for you.

Are there times when just freezing before you act can help? Can it help you to make better choices? Does it give you time to think of the best solution to a tricky problem?

If there are times when a parent or teacher asks you to do something that you don't want to do, it might be wise to pause (**freeze**), think about your reaction to it (**think**) and then respond (**act**). This three-step process might be worth trying.

Why Not Try This?

Divide a lolly stick into three sections.

Write **FREEZE!** in pink, **THINK!** in yellow and **ACT!** in brown.

This can act as a reminder to follow these important steps!

O is for Outer Space

What would we pass if we travelled away from Earth, higher and higher, until we reached outer space?

At approximately 60 miles above the earth you pass through the Kármán line. This is the line at which the mixture of the gases in the atmosphere changes. Gravity changes too and there is no longer enough lift for a normal aircraft to fly any higher!

Then, at an altitude of around 220 miles, you would see the International Space Station (ISS) orbiting around Earth (thanks again to gravity) about every hour and a half! Further up still (340 miles) and you get to the Hubble Space Telescope. This is able to lock on to a target about the width of a human hair at a distance of one mile.

Beyond even the planet Neptune lies a region of more than 100,000 icy rocks, called the Kuiper Belt, that is over two thousand million miles away – now that is outer space, but the sun is still keeping them in orbit!

Whether you call them meteors, planets or asteroids, the universe is full of rocks, with small ones being pulled by medium ones, which in turn are drawn by the gravity of the biggest ones! They all influence each other, just like us! Your friends have an influence on you, and your family do too. But who are the ones who have the biggest positive pull on your thoughts?

Why Not Try This?

Paint three different-sized rocks in grey paint to make them look like meteors.

On the largest write the name of someone who has the biggest influence on you.

Then repeat for the medium and small ones.

Keep them to remind you of the strength they give you when you are feeling pulled down.

P is for Pirate

One of the most treasured phrases of pirate language is the term 'pieces of eight'. It is squawked by Long John Silver's parrot in the book *Treasure Island*. We are told, in Robert Louis Stevenson's story, that the parrot (whose name is Captain Flint) would say, '"Pieces of eight! Pieces of eight!" till you wondered that it was not out of breath'.

So, what were these *pieces of eight*? Well, the title of the book gives us a clue that these 'pieces of eight' were the *Treasure* (the coins in the treasure chest that the pirates were hunting for) on the *Island* (their location, suitably marked on the map with a pirate-like 'X')!

Spanish 'pieces of eight' were minted in both silver (called *reales*) and gold (called *escudos*). If the pirates found them, they would be able to buy anything they wanted in any part of the world at that time. It was the world's first money that everyone accepted as payment for cloth, spices or other goods. Shiver me timbers, who would have thought that!

We all have things that we treasure. It might be treasured time with our family and friends, a good book or a series on TV. Some people call this time 'me time' because we are doing things that make us happy with people we like to be with. It is good to have a mixture of things on this list so that it doesn't get boring; we need to switch between activities and the people we do them with. Sometimes alone, sometimes with others, what's in your 'treasured' chest? Can you think of tricky times when looking at your treasure might help you work through a problem?

Why Not Try This?

Draw round a 2p coin a number of times on a piece of paper.

Inside each circle, write down something that is treasured by you.

Cut them out and stick them on to a number of 2p coins.

Find a box to put them in – your treasured booty.

Or share them with others and get them to make some too.

Return to your treasure when you need a boost.

Q is for Questions

Asking the question 'Why…?' helps you make sense of the world and encourages you to learn new things. Rudyard Kipling, author of the *Just So Stories*, wrote a poem on asking questions about a lady who had 'one million hows, two million wheres and seven million whys'. With ten million questions, this lady will take a long time to answer all of them!

To start, she could ask a **How**, **Why** or **Where** question about these words: Quadriceps, Quagmires or Quidditch.

In the same poem, the author also introduces servants called What, When and Who.

She could then try asking **What**, **When** and **Who** questions about other words that begin with Q – such as Quadruplets, Quesadilla and Quartz?

I think that Mr Kipling may have been on to something, and that being curious and asking about the world in which you live makes it a happier place to be. This makes you interesting and interested. It gives you a sense of purpose and reason, as well as being fun. Everywhere you look should provoke a question that you could discover, research and find the answer to. Keep asking the kind of questions that adults stop asking. After all, the internet makes it much easier! Questions are just one click away, answers are one tap closer, and you are all the stronger for building your skills of exploring and investigating!

Why Not Try This?

Make yourself a dice, but change the six numbers to the six question words.

Go around the house and in each room pick an object.

Use your dice to create the first word of a question about it.

Now try to answer these questions and create a mini-book of your answers.

Share this with people at home and tell them what you have discovered.

R is for Rainbows

The colours of the rainbow are 'Richard (red) Of (orange) York (yellow) Gave (green) Battle (blue) In (indigo) Vain (violet)'. This is called a **mnemonic** — a sentence created to help you remember something.

But are there more than seven colours in a rainbow? Does it go straight from red to orange, or does it move from red into red-oranges and then on to orange? Don't the oranges then become more yellowy until they become yellow and so on…?

In reality, then, you only know some of your rainbow colours. You need to find other names for red-orange, orange-yellow and yellow-green, and then you can create a longer sentence to remember all **13 words** (for all the in-between colours too).

I also thought that rainbows were arc-shaped or semi-circles, as they have always been that shape when I have seen one! However, I am seeing the rainbow from ground level; if I was up in a plane, I'd be looking down at a full-circle rainbow — in seven-plus colours, still in the same order, but in a totally new shape!

It can sometimes seem a bit daunting and not reachable (a bit like the end of a rainbow) when you try to achieve something **BIG**. When faced with these situations, you need to 'think in rainbow colours'; by that, I mean in small, graduated steps. Red looks very different to violet and yet they are only seven steps (or 13 smaller steps) apart. This can make something feel easier to do, and then it is more likely to be done. Asking yourself how you can get to the *next* colour, rather than to the *end* colour, should help.

Why Not Try This?

Create a rainbow plan for something that you really want to achieve.

Draw a simple rainbow and in each of the seven rainbow colours write down an action that you need to take.

(If it is something really **BIG**, then try 13 colours/actions.)

Tick them off as you do them so that you see you are making progress.

S is for Sandcastle

Children and adults alike have been testing their sand-architectural skills since Victorian times. In an old book from 1838, called *Conversations of a Father with His Children*, Papa and his son, William, do exactly that: 'First form a good solid heap of sand; make it round and wide at the bottom… that's right. Now beat it round and make it as hard and as smooth as you can.'

They then put a 'dry stick' flagpole in the top before discussing the benefits of a moat in protecting against the enemy, which I guess is the tide! Victorians' love of sandcastles continued when Bovril sponsored a competition to build the biggest and best sand structure. This clever advertising campaign brought thousands of spectators to the beach to observe this sandy marvel.

In recent times, sandcastles have become modern monuments and you can now be a professional sand sculptor. One rather impressive world-record-worthy 'castle of sand' was 17.65 metres tall, used 11,000 tonnes of sand and took a team of 20 people three and a half weeks to complete.

Papa and William started with a 'good, solid heap of sand' and you too need to build from a solid base. It takes time to get the 'mix' just right to achieve this, but it is worth the effort, because if you do get the consistency right, then you can start to build other castles on top. Without it, the 'incoming tide' will knock it/you down! Your basic needs are to **have good sleep**, and to **eat and drink well**. Focus on building these basic needs and not the 'decorative dry stick' for the top!

Why Not Try This?

Create your own three-layer sandcastle on a piece of sandpaper, then cut it out carefully.

On the bottom tier write words like **SLEEP**, **EAT**, **DRINK**.

Then on the rest write everything else that you can do because you have built this solid base.

T is for Teddy Bear

If I asked you to name a creature that builds a nest, you would be likely to say robin, sparrow or some other bird. However, some bears make nests in the trees too, like the sun bear from Sumatra, or the speckled bear native to South America. Do you know a bear from 'Darkest Peru' in South America? Yes, Paddington Bear is based on the speckled bear, but more about him in another chapter, on wellies.

Originally, teddy bears were based on real bears. With the sun bear being one of the smallest of the bear family, it seemed a good choice for this popular cuddly toy. Despite their name, however, sun bears are nocturnal, meaning that they are active during the night and sleep during the day – the time when the sun is out! Maybe they should have been called moon bears!

The good news is that they have another name too – honey bears. And, like the infamous Winnie the Pooh, they do **LOVE** honey. Indeed, they have specialised long claws for tearing open trees where bees' nests are found. They can then slurp up the runny honey using their extra-long tongues.

A nest is a secure place for birds, bears and bees that allows them to feel comfortable and safe. We all need a home like this – a place where we can recharge ourselves after a busy day at school. It might be your bedroom, it may be the sofa in the sitting room, or possibly the fantasy world of a good book. These are all means of escaping from the busyness of the world in which you live, a time to pause, rest and reflect.

Why Not Try This?

Complete this *acrostic poem* for the **SUN BEAR** using words and phrases about how the bear feels safe in his nest and able to settle down to a much-needed sleep.

Maybe even waking him up in the morning feeling refreshed and happy?

- **S**afely within my twigs and branches

- **U**nder the starry sky, I lie

- **N**esting down for the night

- **B**

- **E**

- **A**

- **R**

Now try writing an acrostic poem using your name.

U is for Unicorn

Narwhals are sea-based creatures that have one horn and yet they don't get nearly as much attention as their mythical cousin, the unicorn. Sometimes called 'the unicorn of the sea', this unique creature has a marvellous spiralling tusk that can grow longer than eight metres. Amazingly, this horn is a very long canine tooth that grows out of its head! In fact, on very rare occasions, both canine teeth grow to create double tusks, but then they can't really be called unicorns of the sea any more!

Presumably, unicorn horns are like the horns of an antelope, which are permanently fixed to the skull (although not actually part of the skull). Antelope horns consist of a bone covered in a layer of keratin, which is the material that builds your hair, birds' feathers and claws, and probably (after all, it is a mythical creature) a unicorn's one horn!

A narwhal's scientific name is 'Monodon monoceros', which means 'one tooth, one horn'. Both 'mono' (Greek) and 'uni' (Latin) mean 'one'. If the unicorn had a science-based name, would it be a 'unique uniceros'? We will never know for sure, as the creature of glitter and rainbows is limited to story books and thus open to imagination and creative thoughts!

Have you ever stopped to think about the ways in which you are unique (the only one)?

What are the unique ingredients that make you **you**? It could be your height, your love of computer games or that you are good at drama. Or it might be that you are also a person who is caring, trustworthy and kind. You are the only one and sometimes we forget this!

Why Not Try This?

Fill a piece of paper with connected triangles (like the pattern in the unicorn drawing).

In each triangle write one thing that you like, one thing that you do or one thing that you are.

Ask a friend or family member to do this too.

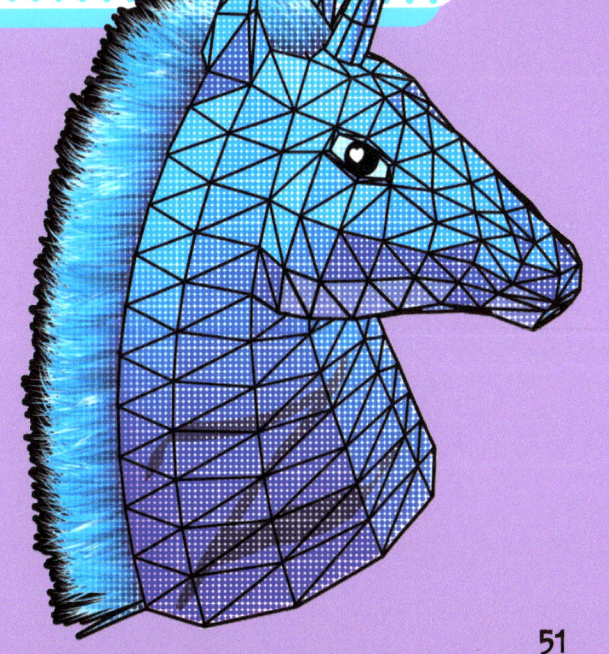

Compare them – are they the same?

V is for Volcano

The word 'volcano' originally comes from the Romans, as they named their god of fire Vulcan. He was actually the god of 'fire and forge' (a workshop where they make things out of metal). The metal has to be heated in a furnace before it can be shaped to become a sword or a helmet.

In Roman mythology, Vulcan was one of the 12 gods in the heavens – those that made up the Council of Gods. In fact, Vulcan had most of his family on the council – with his parents, Juno and Jupiter, and his wife, Venus, also present!

A festival called Vulcanalia was held in honour of Vulcan on 23rd August each year, where citizens offered sacrifices to Vulcan to try to save their grain and food in the fields from harm of fire. In the year 79 CE, the day after the Vulcan festival, Mount Vesuvius, one of the most famous of all volcanoes, started to stir. The full-blown eruption of molten lava, acrid smoke and volcanic ash meant that the sacrifices had not worked and Pompeii, the city closest to the volcano, was all but destroyed.

Do you sometimes feel so angry that you want to explode?

Volcanoes are violent, yet not sudden. They are a gradual build-up of pressure and force. Similarly, your anger may not be as impulsive as you think it is either. We get angry when we let something develop rather than dealing with it – we 'bottle it up' rather than talking about it. It then all comes out in one big explosion, but it can take time to sort out the damage that it causes. You would be wise to work out what makes you go **BANG** and then try to stop it from getting to that stage.

Why Not Try This?

Cut a triangle of toast and take a small bite out of one corner to make the volcano crater.

Use alphabetti spaghetti to create the explosion, spelling out **ANGRY** words with the letters.

W is for Wellies

Bearly Believable is the name of a book about the development of the official Paddington Bear toy. The clothes that we connect with Paddington Bear are his old bush hat (which apparently once belonged to Paddington's uncle, Pastuzo), his duffle coat (which was given to him by his adopted family, the Browns) and his red wellies.

This book reveals that the toy Paddington was not able to stand up, and this was the reason Paddington ended up wearing wellies! In the books, he didn't wear anything on his feet until the toy was produced. The author of the stories, Michael Bond, had to write in a reason for Paddington wearing red wellies, and he decided that he would be given a pair for Christmas.

Such was the popularity of the toy Paddington that the makers struggled to keep up with demand. A company called Dunlop (which we connect with making car tyres) made the wellies for him! Each pair was authenticated with a bear's paw print moulded into the sole, and his initials in the heel: P.B.

Paddington Bear arrived in London with very little; he was found sitting on his suitcase with a note attached to his coat that read, 'Please look after this bear. Thank you.' Many children have cared for their Paddington — hat, coat and wellies too.

Sometimes parents say, 'You need to stand up on your own two feet' — a bit like the Paddington toy. They mean that you need to try to do something yourself without asking for help. As you get older, you become more independent and this is all part of growing up. This is much easier to say than to do. However, if you are brave, then usually you can be surprised by what you can achieve. Just think of how much courage Paddington needed to show, coming to London on his own for the first time.

Why Not Try This?

Draw round your feet on a piece of paper.

Write your own initials in bubble writing on the heels.

In the rest of the foot, write about a time when you did something all on your own for the first time rather than asking for help from someone at school or home.

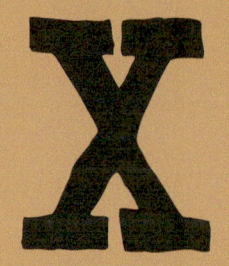

X is for Xenoceratops

If asked to name a dinosaur, most people would say Tyrannosaurus rex, some would say Triceratops and others (who may have seen the Steven Spielberg film *Jurassic Park*) might say Velociraptor. Very few people would pick out Xenoceratops even though it is a cousin to Triceratops (as the two names sharing 'ceratops' suggests)!

In fact, if asked to name a period in history when dinosaurs roamed the earth, most people would say Jurassic, but there was a Triassic period before that, and a Cretaceous period afterwards. Both Triceratops and Xenoceratops come from this later period and yet they are still separated by some 15 million years.

Xenoceratops were 2000-kilogram vegetarians that flourished by eating ferns, cycads and horsetails – plants that were also prospering in this period. Xenoceratops was well armoured for protection against predators, with horns positioned prominently all over the armoured plate that framed the skull of this ancient Canadian creature.

Like Xenoceratops, you need to protect yourself from getting hurt, or 'spiked', by an unkind word or action; angry, or 'spiked', when you are told not to do something; even upset, or 'spiked', with yourself when you don't live up to your own expectations of what you know you can do. All of these can hurt your feelings or make you feel down. If you do get 'spiked', then you need to find help to heal yourself. This can be done by talking with an adult or sharing what happened with a friend.

Why Not Try This?

Use a flattened cereal box to draw a template for a dinosaur mask, like this:

Paint the detail of the Xenoceratops' face on to the coloured side of the card.

On the other side, write some words and phrases to describe moments when:

(a) you have been 'spiked' and
(b) how you protect yourself from being 'spiked'.

Y

is for Yo-Yo

On 12th April 1985, a yo-yo and nine other toys were taken into space on the Space Shuttle Discovery as part of a 'Toys in Space' project.

Would the toys react differently in space?

Would they become extra special and be able to do out-of-this-world things when in orbit?

Seventeen years later, NASA wanted to learn more about how being in a microgravity environment would affect the behaviour of these popular toys, so they returned for more experiments at the International Space Station. Would the Jacob's Ladder still cascade? Would the Flipping Bear still flip? Would the Jumping Frog suction toy still jump?

It was found that the yo-yo must be thrown, not dropped, as there was no gravity to pull it down. That means that you could throw it in any direction, not just downwards. With practice, the astronauts were able to develop new tricks with graceful anti-gravitational movements, all named after space-related things, like Around the World, of course!

The specialist yo-yo that they took to space may have included precision ball bearings inside, but there was also the simple loop at the end of the string. It is this little feature that makes the yo-yo work.

You, like a yo-yo, have that person who has their finger 'in the loop' for you. At times, you are let out, but you can still feel that tug to go back to them every now and again. As you get older, you feel more confident to be let out more, to be increasingly independent. The moments when you feel the tug of the string will become less frequent and that is OK – it is all part of growing up.

Why Not Try This?

Stick a card circle on either end of a cotton reel to create your pretend yo-yo.

Don't forget the all-important loop on the string that you wrap around the reel.

On one circle write all the things that you love to do independently.

On the other write the names of the people who are your person 'in the loop'.

Zzz is for Sleep

Which creature's sleep patterns would you like?

Be a giraffe, as they can even sleep standing up! They can do this by locking their knees, and this allows them to run away quickly when they need to escape from predators – after all, it's a long way from lying down to getting up. Sometimes, they have to risk lying down to give their necks and their bodies a rest – **deep sleep is good**.

A koala then? Thanks to eating all that eucalyptus, they need around 15 hours of sleep every day. Their limited diet has not given them enough energy to do anything else! This long sleep is possible because they can get up high in the trees, safe from predators – **soothing sleep is good**.

Or maybe like an orangutan and other apes, who build platforms that are able to support their sizeable weight. This means that they are safe to sleep for longer, and scientists think that this 'extra sleep' allowed their brains to develop much faster than those of other primates, and they are therefore more intelligent creatures – **sleep is good for your brain**.

Different creatures need different amounts of sleep depending on what they eat and how safe they feel. But all animals need sleep – sleep is **ama-zzzzzzzzzz-ing**.

Unlike our mobile devices, we don't have on/off switches. Like other animals, we need to prepare for sleep. This can be by reading a book, being read a story by someone else, or just dimming the lights. Sleep is a habit and, like other habits we have, some of our sleep habits are good and some of them are not so good.

What are your sleep habits like?

How well do you prepare yourself for sleep, without the bright light of TV or a tablet computer shining in your eyes?

How much sleep do you get a night?

Why Not Try This?

Make a Zzz chart!

Record how many Zs you get each night for a whole week.

Write down one 'Z' for each hour.

Following this rule, how many hours has the koala been sleeping for?

(By the way, have you spotted the ten Zs (the number of hours that you need to try to get each night) that have been hidden in the other pictures in the book?)

of related interest

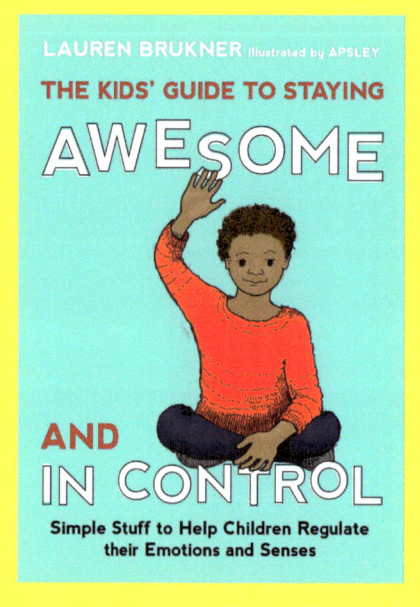

THE KIDS' GUIDE TO STAYING AWESOME AND IN CONTROL
Simple Stuff to Help Children Regulate their Emotions and Senses
Lauren Brukner, Illustrated by Apsley

ISBN 978 1 84905 997 8
eISBN 978 0 85700 962 3

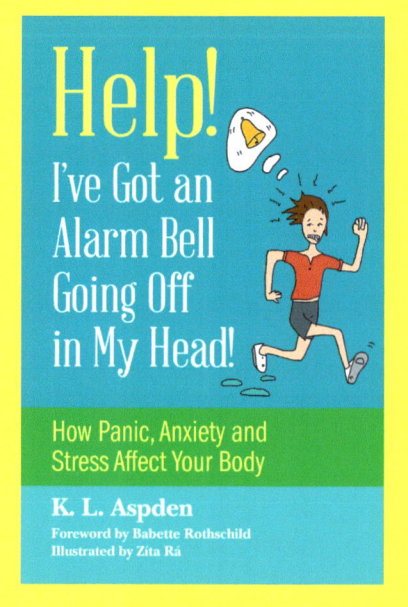

Help! I've Got an Alarm Bell Going Off in My Head!
How Panic, Anxiety and Stress Affect Your Body
K. L. Aspden
Foreword by Babette Rothschild
Illustrated by Zita Rá

ISBN 978 1 84905 704 2
eISBN 978 1 78450 227 0

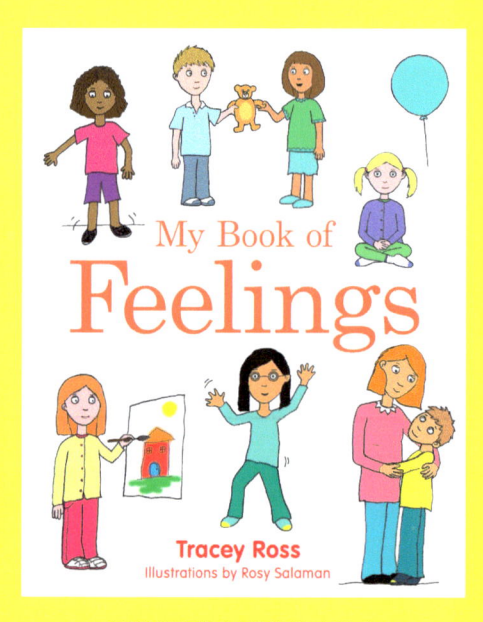

My Book of Feelings
Tracey Ross
Illustrations by Rosy Salaman

ISBN 978 1 78592 192 6
eISBN 978 1 78450 466 3

The solution to the problem on page 31 is VI.